Published by SL Resources, Inc.
A Division of Student Life

© 2009 SL Resources, Inc.

Student Life
Attn: Ministry Resources
2183 Parkway Lake Drive
Birmingham, AL 35226

ISBN-10: 1935040227
ISBN-13: 978-1935040224

31 Verses Every Teenager Should Know™

www.studentlife.com
www.31verses.com

Printed in the United States of America

31

verses

EVERY TEENAGER
SHOULD KNOW

table of contents

INTRO

So, what's the deal with flip?

Well, all the way back at the very beginning of your Bible, God created a perfect world. So, what happened? We decided to do the opposite of what God said. Only one tree was off limits, and you know the rest. We not only plucked the forbidden fruit, we took a big juicy bite and passed it around . . . everything has been out of balance ever since. Life seems to spin out of control.

But God is still in control. His Word (your Bible) tells us over and over again to trust Him. It warns us against the backward desire of our sinful nature, calls us to turn around, and invites us to join the King as He flips everything right side up again. God's way of doing things won't always make sense. Just look at the rest of the story. Since mankind left the garden, God has moved in unexpected ways through unlikely heroes: a stuttering prophet, a giant-slaying youth, a pregnant virgin; and ultimately God Himself came as the Servant King and crucified Savior.

So, what about you? As a Christ-follower, you can't just go with the flow . . . everything is swirling down the drain. It's easy to get sucked in and swept away if we're not intentional about holding tight to the truth of the gospel. The Kingdom of God is in direct opposition to this fallen world. Following Christ is counter-cultural. It flies in the face of so-called common sense. Your friends, your family, even your church may think you've gone crazy when your life starts moving in a new direction.

Andy and I hope you do lose your mind . . . meaning you replace your thoughts with the Word, your plans with God's will, and your life with Christ's Kingdom.

Let this book flip your world around . . .

Fellow Traveler Along the Way,

Jeremy Maxfield
Writer and Editor

Now that you own this incredible little book, you may be wondering, "What do I do with it?"

Glad you asked. The great thing about this book is that you can use it just about any way you want.

It's not a system. It's a resource that can be used in ways that are as unique and varied as you are.

A few suggestions . . .

HOW

USE

The One Month Plan
On this plan, you'll read one devotional each day for a month. This is a great way to immerse yourself in the Bible for a month-long period. (OK, we realize that every month doesn't have 31 days. But 28 or 30 is close enough to 31, right?) The idea is to cover a lot of information in a short amount of time.

The Scripture Memory Plan
The idea behind this plan is to memorize the verse for each day's devotional; you don't move on to the next devotional until you've memorized the Scripture you're on. If you're like most people, this might take you more than one day per devotional. So this plan takes a slower approach.

The "I'm No William Shakespeare" Plan
Don't like to write or journal? This plan is for you. . . . Listen, not everyone expresses themselves the same way. If you don't like to express yourself through writing, that's OK. Simply read the devotional for each verse, then read the questions. Think about them. Pray through them. But don't feel as if you have to journal if you don't want to.

The Strength in Numbers Plan
God designed humans for interaction. We're social creatures. How cool would it be if you could go through 31: Flip with your friends? Get a group of friends together. Consider agreeing to read five verses each week, then meeting to talk about them.

Pretty simple, right? Choose a plan. Or make up your own. But get started already. What are you waiting for?

VERSE

In 1931, New York City marveled as the Empire State Building pierced the clouds at 1,250 feet, holding the title World's Tallest Skyscraper for 41 years. America's ingenuity seemed limitless; nothing would keep us from achieving our goals. By the late 60s, NASA was launching people 240,000 miles off the face of our planet, leaving human footprints in moon dust. Right now, an American satellite is hurtling through space farther than any manmade object in history. But even at 10.1 billion miles away, Voyager 1 needs to travel that distance almost 7 trillion more times to reach what our best telescopes have seen (so far). WHAT?!?!? My point is that no matter how big we build something, how smart we get, or how far we explore, God is infinitely greater.

Read Isaiah 55. Even though Isaiah wrote these words 700 years before Christ, his book contains some of the most precise prophecies concerning the Suffering Servant and Savior of God's people (go back later and check out chapter 53 to see what I mean). In today's Scripture, God reminds us that His wisdom and ability are worlds beyond ours. God is so powerful that even His words are on a spiritual mission from heaven and never return without accomplishing His plan. His truth turns everything around, bringing life, joy, and peace out of sin, selfishness, and suffering.

Sometimes we just don't understand God. In fact, He often does the exact opposite of what we would do. That's ok! If we always understood God, He would be small and simple enough to fit into our minds, right? God is HUGE. As great as our minds and accomplishments may be, only God truly knows best. Only He can give us a life beyond anything we ever imagined. Starting now, let's stop relying on our own thinking and allow God's Word to flip our world around!

REFLECT

1. What are some things that you just don't understand about God? Write them here. Pray that God would give you a peace about trusting Him with these things.

2. How would keeping God's greatness in the front of your mind affect your thoughts, attitudes, and actions?

3. God's Word is powerful. It will change your life. That's a promise. Write down the time and place that you will commit to reading Scripture each day, including the rest of this book.

VERSE

IN REPLY JESUS DECLARED, "I TELL YOU THE TRUTH, NO ONE
CAN SEE THE KINGDOM OF GOD UNLESS HE IS BORN AGAIN."
John 3:3

During each episode of MythBusters© on the Discovery Channel™, the
hosts perform experiments aimed at proving or disproving the weird and
wacky things some people believe. This is both entertaining and helpful
since it's sometimes hard to know the difference between fact and fiction.
Have you seen the one about cell phones and gas stations? One myth is
that if you answer your phone while pumping gas . . . BOOM! You could
be saying hello to a fiery mushroom cloud. Supposedly, electronic devices
and flammable fumes have a potentially explosive relationship. There's also
the risk of recreating the gas station fiasco in your stomach by downing Pop
Rocks® and soft drinks. Fortunately, the goal of MythBusters is to set the
record straight on such claims.

In a greater way, Jesus entered the world to set the record straight on the
all-important issue of God's Kingdom. People cannot afford to be confused
about the way of salvation (entering His Kingdom). In John 3:1-16, a
religious leader named Nicodemus came at night seeking clarity on Jesus'
relationship to the Kingdom of God. Like a lot of people, Nicodemus
believed the myth that religion was the way of salvation—by being born into
the right family, obeying God's Law, and doing the right things. But Jesus
flipped the script on Nicodemus and said that life with God doesn't come
through religion but rebirth.

There is a night and day difference between religion and rebirth. Religion
teaches salvation by becoming a "better" person by going to youth group and
staying out of trouble. Rebirth involves becoming a new person by going to
Jesus. Ultimately, religion leaves people in the dark; rebirth brings people
into the light. In rebirth, the Holy Spirit turns the light on in a person's
life so he or she can see Jesus and follow Him into God's Kingdom.

1. What myths have you heard about life, God, and the way of salvation? (things people believe but they aren't true)

2. Why do you think people believe they can enter God's Kingdom through religious activities? How are you living like that myth is true? How are you "busting" it?

3. Are you a reborn Christ-follower? Does your faith rest in Him or in your religious activities? Why?

4

verse **3**

ON HEARING THIS, JESUS SAID TO THEM, "IT IS NOT THE
HEALTHY WHO NEED A DOCTOR, BUT THE SICK. I HAVE
NOT COME TO CALL THE RIGHTEOUS, BUT SINNERS."
Mark 2:17

Walking into a school cafeteria is like walking into a department store. It doesn't matter if it's Saks Fifth Avenue or T.J. Maxx®, department stores are organized into categories: men's, women's, fragrance, shoes, etc. Shoppers won't find a Louis Vuitton® handbag mixed in with the Nike® Shox, although some girls would make a mad dash to get their hands on these designer bags! Likewise, tables in a school cafeteria are often divided into sections: the football table, the cheerleading table, the gamer table, the studious table, the band table, and others. Seated at separate tables are groups of students who look and act a lot like each other. Often times, sitters at the respective tables don't mix and mingle. If Jesus attended your school, at what table would He eat? Would He only eat with those who were like Him, at the Son of God table?

Read Mark 2:15-17. Seated around Jesus' table were many people who were different from Him. Sinners and tax collectors were a mixed bag of social outcasts. Sharing a meal with someone in His day represented a special time of fellowship. The religious elite despised the makeup of Jesus' lunch table. To the Pharisees, associating with such "losers" was unthinkable. They hated Jesus and made fun of Him for befriending unpopular people, yet Jesus never folded under their pressure. Instead, He gladly risked His reputation for the sake of redemption.

Jesus' redemptive reach extended beyond all social boundaries. He wasn't ashamed to associate with anyone—regardless of differences. The call of the Christ-follower is to approach life the same way. It's easy to avoid people not like us. Sometimes we may even catch ourselves judging others as "bad people," but aren't they exactly the people who need their lives flipped by God's grace?

REFLECT

1. Honestly, are you willing to risk your reputation for the sake of redemption? Why or why not?

2. What types of people do you have a hard time loving? Why? Take some time and ask God to change your heart toward such people.

3. List two students from your school who are often overlooked and may not have any friends. How might you befriend them and show them the love of Christ?

VERSE
4

Pain and suffering are frequent companions in life's journey and affect
people in a variety of ways. For Nick Vujicic, life had always been difficult,
physically and emotionally. He was constantly bullied, made fun of, and
stared at because he was born without arms or legs. As a child, Nick would
pray desperately for God to grow him new limbs. God didn't answer Nick's
prayer for arms and legs in this life, but He did give him hope and a pur-
pose for living. This young Australian has found joy in the middle of his
trials through faith in Christ. Vujicic knows that someday everything will
be made new, but today, he'll make the most of every opportunity to share
hope through smiles, speaking, and even surfing.

Read Revelation 21:1-8. The book of Revelation is a book of hope for
pain-stricken Christ-followers. Throughout the book, the sufferings of
life are intensely displayed in a variety of ways: natural disasters, famines,
diseases, persecutions, and broken relationships. All of these sufferings
are experienced often in this world, yet all the while the hope of heaven is
before people reminding Christ-followers that their pain is temporary and
will give way to an eternity of joy with Jesus. Sin, suffering, and Satan have
an expiration date.

Unlike Nick's mysterious situation, we know what causes our condition:
sin. The world is broken, fractured by sin, and so is everybody who lives
in it. We're born into the middle of a mixed-up order of things. Bullies,
loneliness, and insecurities get us bent out of shape; disease, divorce, and
death are all painful realities. But there is hope! Jesus Christ will set all
things right. He is our hope. A new reality awaits for all who overcome this
life through His strength.

reflect

1. What have you cried about lately?

2. Do you tend to turn to Jesus or away from Him in the midst of pain? Why?

3. Write down a situation that is currently painful. How might the truth that pain is temporary and joy with Jesus is eternal affect your experience with life's difficulties?

VERSE

"COME NOW, LET US REASON TOGETHER,"
SAYS THE LORD. "THOUGH YOUR SINS ARE
LIKE SCARLET, THEY SHALL BE AS WHITE
AS SNOW; THOUGH THEY ARE RED AS
CRIMSON, THEY SHALL BE LIKE WOOL."

Isaiah 1:18

"Silence the stain, instantly." This was the tagline for the Super Bowl® XLII ad voted #1 on YouTube™. In 2008, Tide® to Go ran a commercial featuring an obnoxious spot that began shouting gibberish each time the owner of the stained shirt spoke. The poor guy realized that his job interview was bombing because the interviewer was completely distracted by the loud-mouthed blob. All efforts to present himself worthy of consideration were completely overshadowed by his sloppy nemesis. The stain grew louder each time the applicant attempted to plead his case, until he finally gave up hopeless. If only something could remove stains, making you presentable and as good as new.

The prophet Isaiah opened his book with a similar dilemma. Read Isaiah 1:11-18. Israel had a major problem. God was completely disgusted by their so-called religious activities. He even said that He hated their worship rituals, their offerings were worthless, and He could not listen to their prayers. Wow. Why would God say something so shocking? Israel was deeply stained with sin. They continued to go through the motions, pretending like nothing was wrong. Unless they ridded themselves of this evil and guilt, nothing they did to look good could overcome the selfish demands of their sin-soaked hearts.

Fortunately for us, there is hope. Jesus Christ is the One Isaiah promised would wash away our sins, cleansing us and making a relationship with God possible. Only through Him can we be forgiven and made new. Even our best efforts are useless, empty routines of meaningless noise. God takes our hearts and flips them inside out, removing every spot and blemish, so that we can live in His will. Our situation can change. We can do the right things. He will make us new, silencing the stain, instantly.

REFLECT

1. Spiritually, how have you been going through the motions and possibly offending God (and others) with your talking stain?

2. Pray now. Don't selfishly ask God for things you want. Ask Him to show you the sins that need to be removed from your life. Ask Christ to wash you clean of those stains. He will.

3. Write your sins in the shape of a cross. Then color over them so only the cross is visible on a blank page. This is your new life.

VERSE 6

"THE TIME HAS COME," HE SAID. "THE KINGDOM OF GOD IS NEAR. REPENT AND BELIEVE THE GOOD NEWS!"
Mark 1:15

ZOMBIES AHEAD. Silently screaming in massive orange letters, the unexpected message jolted morning commuters awake. You know they laughed then checked their door locks, a little jumpy with any sudden movements for the rest of the drive. January 19, 2009, someone hacked into a computerized road sign designed to communicate emergency instructions for redirecting traffic. The sign prepares people for what they will encounter if continuing in their current direction. This warning message of what was coming in the near future was so bizarre that nobody took it seriously—not admittedly, at least!

Read Mark 1:14-20. Throughout history, God used prophets (and now the Bible) to guide people in the right direction. Here, Jesus began His ministry with the same message as John the Baptist. "Repent" means to turn around, 180 degrees, because your sin is leading you down a dangerous path. Jesus called these disciples to stop what they were doing, turn around, believe, and follow Him. No matter how unexpected this message was, these men were willing to change the course of their lives to experience a future in God's Kingdom.

Like zombies who walk around but have no real life, Scripture says we are dead in our sin. The good news is that we have been warned and shown where to go for new life. Actually, the new life came to us. The directions for entering the Kingdom of God are simple: repent and believe the gospel. Jesus says that the time is now. Turn away from sin, trust God, and go in any direction He shows you. Paying attention to this message will save you from going down a dead end road. It may sound crazy, but it's true. Christ has brought God's future Kingdom into the middle of our lives today. Will you take Him seriously?

1. "I am already saved," you may think, so you skimmed through this devotion. If you did, reread this. Ask God to show you some things that you still need to turn away from.

2. Write down the names of some friends who do not yet believe the gospel. How can God work through your life to show them His Kingdom?

3. What would be different if the whole world lived like God was King over everything? Does this sound impossible? It starts right now in your own heart. Pray that God would be honored as King in your life.

FOR WHOEVER WANTS TO SAVE HIS LIFE WILL LOSE IT, BUT
WHOEVER LOSES HIS LIFE FOR ME AND FOR THE GOSPEL
WILL SAVE IT.
Mark 8:35

Have you ever played competitive sports? Any committed athlete will
tell you that when you are part of a team, life is no longer about you
as an individual. A serious coach will lead a player through rigorous
training that impacts every area of the athlete's life. Everything is sacrificed for a greater cause: winning as a team. They are part of something bigger than themselves and are willing to give anything to see the
team advance victoriously. That's just a game, so what about life?

Anyone enthusiastic about following Christ may think twice about
doing so after reading Mark 8:34-38. Jesus warned that the disciple's
road would be marked by sacrifice. Those who join His team must
surrender their lives completely to His leadership. In so doing, they
embrace the possibility of persecution and, perhaps, death. But with
the warning comes the reward—Jesus promised His disciples that for
them even death was not the end. Surrendering their lives to Jesus was
worth any personal loss. Nothing in this world is more valuable than
the reward gained by those enduring for the sake of God's Kingdom.

Today, there are still shocking and inspiring stories of martyrs refus-
ing to compromise. But long before any of those people literally lost
their lives, they made a choice to give up living for themselves; eternal
reward far outweighed any personal sacrifice. Most of us will never
face martyrdom, literally dying for our faith, but how many of us
are even living for what we believe? Although Christians in America
don't face the threat of persecution, we do face the temptation of
self-preservation. Promoting Christ in our schools and communities
means losing our "own life" in order to experience His. We live for
the reward of the Kingdom instead of personal success, comfort, or
popularity.

1. Are you more worried about preserving your popularity or promoting Christ and His cause? How are you saving your life? How are you losing it for Christ?

2. What fears keep you from openly talking about the gospel at school?

3. Promoting Christ involves not only talking about Him but also making choices (sometimes hard ones). Take some time to ask the Lord what choices you need to make to better promote Christ and His cause through your life. Write those down.

VERSE 8

BUT SEEK FIRST HIS KINGDOM AND HIS RIGHTEOUSNESS, AND ALL
THESE THINGS WILL BE GIVEN TO YOU AS WELL. *Matthew 6:33*

Many hikers need to be rescued each year because they leave their com-
passes at home. Without a compass, hikers easily lose their bearings and
wind up wandering aimlessly through the wilderness. If you have ever been
hiking, you know how easy it is to lose your sense of direction. Trees and
trails begin to look a lot alike. The weather changes unexpectedly. Clouds
set in and cover the sun, keeping it from being used as a reliable source for
navigation. So much fear and worry could have been avoided if only hikers
had a compass! A compass is the most reliable instrument for navigating
through unfamiliar territory. It always points north regardless of how the
hiker's surroundings may change.

Matthew 6:25-34 is at the center of Jesus' Sermon on the Mount, which
is His most thorough teaching on what it means to be a citizen in God's
Kingdom. In this passage, He reminded the disciples that joy-squashing
fear and anxiety was avoidable by pointing northward, by keeping their faith
focused on God. Panic and stress creep in when citizens of God's Kingdom
turn their attention away from God and focus on the shifting landscape of
their circumstances.

The Christ-follower is like a hiker wandering through the wilderness of
this world. All the while, God intends to be the most reliable source of
navigation in his or her life. God promises to protect and to provide for
His people. As long as a Christ-follower keeps pointing northward, joy will
not be replaced by fear and anxiety. We lose our bearings in life when seeking God and His will no longer takes top priority. Fretting over circumstances actually reflects a lack of trust in God. Matthew 6:33 encourages the
believer to keep pointing northward regardless of the situation.

15

reflect

1. What do you worry about the most?

2. Do you trust God to provide for all your needs? Why or why not?

3. What tends to distract you from pursuing God and His standard of living? Pray about how you can stay focused spiritually.

VERSE

What do World of Warcraft®, Call of Duty®, and Guitar Hero® all have in common? If your eyes are bloodshot from energy drinks and way too much time in front of a screen, you may recognize these super-addictive games. They're all part of the Activision® Blizzard gaming empire. Here's the shocking twist: Bobby Kotick, the President and CEO of this multi-billion dollar company, hates video games. He thinks they're a waste of time! Bobby is a businessman in the truest sense. He's looking to make a buck (or billions of them) by taking advantage of people willing to pay for something that they are passionate about.

What if a similar mindset ever crept into something that truly mattered? Read Matthew 21:12-17. The humble Servant King exhibited His authority, flipping tables and chairs and chasing profiteers out of the crowded Temple courts. The religious system had become entrenched in regulations for who could make what sacrifices, when, where, and how. People had to trade for the right kind of money or buy appropriate sacrifices. Passionate experiences relating to God had turned into opportunities to make a buck. Worship turned into business. People were taken advantage of or excluded in the name of power and profit. Christ welcomed and healed those who had not previously been worthy: the poor, the sick, and the young. When challenged, Jesus simply turned to Scripture.

This powerful display of authority was also a symbolic cleansing of our lives. Christ flipped the greedy distractions and corrupt practices of the world, making room for everyone desiring to worship God. People all around us are still being left out. Others are twisting the Christian life to look more like the world than God's Kingdom. What about you, your friends, your youth group, or your church? Are you turning to Scripture, lifting true praise, and welcoming everyone?

REFLECT

REFLECT

1. How would Jesus react if He were to walk into your church? Would you be chased out or welcomed in?

2. What in your life needs to be flipped? Where are you greedy, manipulative, or exclusive? Pray for change.

3. What can you do to flip a situation? Is someone left out, hurting, put-down, or is there a group with wrong priorities/values? Write down what action you can take to make things right at church, school, work, or home.

VERSE 10

BECAUSE HE HIMSELF SUFFERED WHEN HE WAS TEMPTED, HE
IS ABLE TO HELP THOSE WHO ARE BEING TEMPTED.
Hebrews 2:18

So there's been about a jillion episodes of MADE© on MTV® by now. Why not let everyone in on the action, right? So, wannabemade.com was born. It's a cool concept: you post your goals, others adopt you and become your coach, and everyone can track your progress. There's one major difference, however. Instead of celebrity experts giving you insider tips for success out of their own professional experiences, you get anybody and everybody who has an opinion. They may have good intentions, but if you're trying to land that fakie 360 flip, you're more likely to end up in the ER than the X Games.

Stay with me now. Check out Hebrews 2:18. Hebrews is a deep book with a lot of intimidating words, but here's the deal. This letter was written to demonstrate Christ's superiority to the Jewish Law and sacrificial system of temples and priests. Life was tough, and Christ-followers were growing lonely. Going back to the friends and families that held on to their former religious traditions surely crossed people's minds. But however well intentioned, Judaism had become a common routine of moral advice rather than a direct relationship with the Creator God.

Hebrews encourages us not to give up, no matter what we're dealing with. God knows exactly what we're feeling. I know there was no pill popping, Internet pop-ups, or other popular temptations recently introduced by technology, but Christ was tempted in every way. Jesus suffered through it (meaning it wasn't easy even for Him). He's the expert. Christ experienced a perfect life, never giving in to temptation. Now, we're invited to be made into His image, with His help. This isn't a one-episode deal and then we're on our own, either. We've been adopted, eternally. Christ is our coach, everyday.

1. Who and/or what do you rely on most for advice, encouragement, and accountability? What does this tell you about life goals you are setting?

2. How are you intentionally working to avoid and overcome temptation? What roles are Christ and the Bible playing in your progress?

3. Write down some specific goals relating to temptation. Pray for the wisdom, strength, and courage of Christ in daily accomplishments.

"WHY DO YOU LOOK AT THE SPECK OF SAWDUST IN YOUR
BROTHER'S EYE AND PAY NO ATTENTION TO THE PLANK IN
YOUR OWN EYE?" *Matthew 7:3*

Five words haunted Ralphie Parker: "You'll shoot your eye out!" They
echo throughout A Christmas Story© so often they're practically an
alternate title. Everyone, including Santa Claus, dashed the poor kid's
hopes and dreams for an official, Red Ryder®, carbine-action, 200
shot, range model, air rifle. So what happens after his dad surprises
even Ralphie's mom by giving the nine-year-old the coveted BB gun?
The first shot ricocheted, breaking his glasses, and a story involving a
rogue icicle is quickly devised to cover up the shameful irony.

Check out the imagery Jesus used in Matthew 7:1-5 to warn against
judging others. If your Bible has red letters, you can't miss the fact that
these pages are covered with Christ's teachings. All of the Kingdom
principles, like this one, involve some kind of flipside or unexpected
contrast. Here, we learn that we're in no position to be shooting dirty
looks and pointing fingers in condemnation at anyone. Judgment
bounces right back onto us in a vicious cycle of ricocheting standards
where everyone is hurt. This does NOT mean we ignore sin, looking
the other way since "nobody's perfect." Rather, we need to change our
perspective and priority to examine our own lives first. He even says
to help others, just do so after being honest in dealing with your own
issues.

Ironically, Christ-followers should be known as a loving community,
but we're often seen as judgmental hypocrites. Not a lot has changed
since Jesus' day. Usually, pointing out other people's problems is a
way to avoid our own. We need to admit when we're hurting and what
wounded us. Like Ralphie, sometimes we'll confess something, but
only out of fear for some other "big" sin being discovered. If we understand God's grace, we'll confess our own sins and start seeing each
other through completely different eyes.

1. Stop pretending like you're fine. There's some big, ridiculous sin wedged into your life that needs to be removed. Ask God to show you the plank that you're blind to. Start removing it by writing it down.

2. Write down some things that you know you are judgmental about.

3. Identify a friend or someone you look up to that can help you identify and deal with planks and specks in your life.

VERSE
12

"How much you want to make a bet I can throw a football over those mountains? Yeah. If coach would've put me in fourth quarter, we'd have been state champions, no doubt. No doubt in my mind. You better believe things would have been different. I'd have gone pro . . . in a heartbeat. I'd be making millions of dollars and livin' in a big ol' mansion somewhere. You know, soakin' it up in a hot tub with my soul mate." Uncle Rico in Napoleon Dynamite© hasn't made much progress in life. Stuck in 1982, he's now pushing 40 and still dreaming about what could've been. Because his life is spent looking backward, he's not really living at all. Too many regrets have him stuck in a rut, never moving on, so he's not going anywhere.

Jesus cautioned Christ-followers against looking backward in Luke 9:57-62. In this passage, three potential disciples approached Jesus; only, they choose not to follow him after learning of the radical requirements for being a Christ-follower. Candidate #1 couldn't let go of his dream for a cozy life. Candidate #2 couldn't prioritize Christ's cause over all other obligations. Candidate #3 failed to recognize the superiority of his relationship with Jesus to every other relationship. Because they feared regretting the changes Christ would make in their lives, they weren't fit for service in God's Kingdom.

Christ-followers can't live like regret-stricken Uncle Rico. We've counted the cost and considered any other life to be a rut that we don't want to get stuck in. We've abandoned our dreams, submitted our obligations, and surrendered our relationships to the superiority of Christ and His cause. Anything threatening to divide our devotion to Jesus, causing us to look backward, has been dropped at the gate of God's Kingdom. We believe serving Christ is the most meaningful option we have in life.

reflect

1. Are you tempted to regret your decision to follow Jesus? How might you resist such a temptation so you do not fall into a rut?

2. What threatens to divide your devotion to Christ and His cause? (for example, extracurricular activities, a boyfriend/girlfriend, planning a future without consulting Jesus, lazy summers, etc.)

3. Ask the Lord what changes in priorities need to be made in order for you to be a more devoted and sincere Christ-follower.

VERSE

People do crazy things to get attention. Consider the prideful delusions during American Idol® auditions. The most outrageous thing about American Idol rejects, is that they seriously believe they deserve to be famous. They think they are the best. Season 6 had "Eccentric," the man-panther who claimed to be the single most electrifying entertainer in the world! He proceeded to crawl and growl like a jungle cat while slashing his "paw" through the air—all in an effort to get America's attention. He got it all right. The judges laughed him right off the stage. Thinking so highly of himself and drawing attention to himself actually pushed everyone away. Many things are capable of getting people's attention, both good and bad, but have you ever wondered what grabs God's attention?

James 4:10 reminds readers that humility grabs God's attention. In James 4:1-10, James confronted a group of Christ-followers who had lost sight of this essential truth. They had allowed pride and envy to creep in and corrupt their community. Relationships were on the rocks. No one was getting along because pride made everyone jealous of one another. Consequently, close fellowship with God was scarce. Pride prefers people's attention to God's. On the flip side, humility prefers the pleasure of God's presence. Humbling yourself means you're more interested in people recognizing how amazing God is than how great you are.

Prideful delusions creep into our own lives, causing us to do crazy things to get the attention we think we deserve. Only, we're not always successful. Soon someone else comes along wearing cooler clothes, making better grades, or driving a faster car. Suddenly we're overlooked and unnecessarily angry. Ultimately, only one person's attention matters—God's. Humility always succeeds. While pride stiff-arms God, holding Him at a distance, humility hangs on to Him, craving His closeness.

25

REFLECT

1. What is the difference between pride and humility?

2. Whose attention do you tend to crave most—people's or God's? How?

3. Does conflict consistently characterize your relationships with other people? Take some time and honestly consider whether or not this is the result of pride in your life. If so, confess your pride to God, and ask Him to foster humility within you.

VERSE 14

DO TO OTHERS AS YOU WOULD HAVE THEM DO TO YOU.
Luke 6:31

You know that super-dramatic scene in a movie where a character gets punched in the face, but instead of getting all scared, spastic, or aggressive, they just turn slowly back to look their attacker in the eyes? It's pure strength. Whoever started the fight knows that the table has been turned. The would-be victim is in control, regardless of whatever else is happening. They are choosing to stand up for something bigger than the circumstance, no matter what the personal cost, and the instigator has a moment of realization that their opponent has been underestimated.

Turn to Luke 6, and read verses 27 to 35. Christ was scrolling through a list of unexpected reactions to bad situations. His followers were told to do the exact opposite of how they might expect to respond naturally. Surprise an enemy with love. Flip hateful attitudes with good actions. Swap curses with blessings. Trade abuse for prayer. Take a stand when someone wants to knock you down. Give generously when someone tries to steal, sue, or take advantage of you.

The Golden Rule is buried in the middle of this list. It's not so much about being nice so that others will be nice back; it's about choosing to do what's right even when people do the wrong things to us. It means always living for God's great love and mercy no matter what, even if there's no personal benefit.

To live counter-culturally means to do the opposite of what seems natural. It takes strength; it's not easy. Christ-followers have to stand up for God's Kingdom, reaching out to others with the attitude of Christ. We have to actively share the love of God with the people around us who may want nothing to do with it. Our hope is for a moment of realization, that God's Kingdom has been underestimated.

27

1. To whom do you need to be most intentional about showing God's love (because it is not natural for you to love them)? Write names. Pray now for those people.

2. In what situations do you find yourself reacting selfishly, angrily, or defensively? How will you commit to flipping your attitude in those environments?

3. How does it change your attitude toward other people knowing that even though you sin against God, ignore what He says, and take your relationship for granted, Christ came to love, forgive, and die for you, giving you a new life?

DO NOT BE ANXIOUS ABOUT ANYTHING, BUT IN EVERY-
THING, BY PRAYER AND PETITION, WITH THANKSGIVING,
PRESENT YOUR REQUESTS TO GOD. *Philippians 4:6*

I want you to have a mental picture of this guy George. Think 1800s,
but imagine this white-haired old man rockin' a David Beckham
fauxhawk and Abe Lincoln beard. Google™ it if you don't believe me.
Besides his unique style, George Müller is best known for his pray-
instead-of-worry lifestyle. With only 50 cents in his pocket, George
felt lead to start an orphanage, among other things, funded entirely by
prayer. Not once did he solicit any support. Orphans may be seated at
an empty table when someone walked in to donate food. Nobody ever
missed a meal, and there was never any debt. During Müller's lifetime,
millions of dollars were donated and thousands of orphans cared for,
simply because he prayed instead of worrying.

Read Philippians 4:4-9. The Apostle Paul also lived radically, trusting God even when it seemed crazy. Missionary journeys took Paul
throughout Europe and the Middle East; the church in Philippi was the
first one he actually started. Here, Paul encouraged his friends to lead
prayerful, humble, and content lives, no matter what their individual
circumstances. (FYI: Paul was writing this from prison!) Throughout
his letter, the key is to be focused on God rather than self.

Christ-followers are called to flip our worries into prayers and praise.
When we do this, God turns our anxiety into a peace that doesn't
make sense. I don't mean we shouldn't care; we just can't get wrecked
over things. Anxiety comes from feeling like we can't keep life under
control… and we can't. But God can. Instead of letting our minds race
frantically, chasing all of the pressures and potential disasters in our
schedule, let's practice focusing our minds on God and all the good
things today. What kind of difference will it make in our lives (and
maybe the world) if we would pray instead of worry?

REFLECT

1. Worry is the opposite of prayer. Write down what you worry about. Every time you start to worry about these things today, stop and pray instead.

2. Now, write down things you are thankful for. Don't stop writing until this list is longer than your list of worries. How will you practice dwelling on these things?

3. God is with you. How does this fact affect your thoughts and attitude? Pray that God will remind you of His presence and His blessings whenever you start to worry.

VERSE 16

FOR I DESIRE STEADFAST LOVE, NOT SACRIFICE, THE KNOWLEDGE OF
GOD RATHER THAN BURNT OFFERINGS. *Hosea 6:6*

Sorry girls, but some guys celebrate Valentine's Day half-heartedly. They go through the motions of the pink and red holiday insincerely, without the emotions. Sure they buy their Valentine chocolate and roses, but when asked why, some reply, "That's what the guy's supposed to do."

Sorry guys, but when word of this attitude gets out, you probably won't have to worry about next year. Most girls don't want a Valentine's gift given out of a sense of obligation. They don't want boys going through the motions without the emotions. Sincerity matters on February 14.

As important as sincerity may be on Valentine's Day, it's unquestionably more important when the worship of God is involved. In Hosea 6:4-6, God confronted Israel's half-hearted worship. They had reduced worship to an empty routine—going through the motions without the emotions. In verse 4, God compared their love to the dew on the ground that quickly evaporates every morning. Although they appeared to draw near to God in worship, their hearts have dried up. In a sense, they say, "We worship God not because we love Him but because that's what's expected from us." Regardless of how important sacrifices and burnt offerings were, they remained worthless if presented by people who didn't have sincere love. (Some Bibles translate this word for love as "loyalty" or "mercy.")

As Christ-followers, we don't offer sacrifices and burnt offerings today because Jesus' life, death, and resurrection made them unnecessary. Instead, we offer our lives to God and can do many things to worship Him. We can sing, study Scripture, pray, give food to the poor, paint, journal, do homework, exercise, etc. Any activity qualifies as worship if it honors God and is performed by a person who loves Him. On the flip side, nothing qualifies as worship if a person's heart is indifferent toward God. Sincerity matters.

reflect

1. Why does sincerity of heart matter in worship? How would you describe whole-hearted worship?

2. Do you feel like you're going through the motions of the Christian life without the emotions? If so, don't feel like you're abnormal, but don't settle for the dryness. What might you do to get through a dry season? You can begin by repeatedly asking God to give you a sincere heart to worship Him.

3. How might you express love for God today? Write down some ideas.

VERSE

SO, BECAUSE YOU ARE
LUKEWARM—NEITHER HOT NOR
COLD—I AM ABOUT TO SPIT YOU
OUT OF MY MOUTH.
Revelation 3:16

It's impossible! Whatever . . . I bet I can do it! You know the routine. Confidence melts away in nauseating agony. There's no better
way to shake up that middle-of-the-night boredom at your best
friend's house (notice I didn't say your own house) than the chug-
a-gallon-of-milk-in-an-hour challenge. It seems so easy, and,
at first, it looks that way. But you've never experienced anything
like the wrenching velocity of curdled defeat. Let's just say, I hope
you're outside when you "lose the bet." The force in which nature's
rejection comes spewing forth is mind blowing. Imagine Godzilla
zapping skyscrapers but with blasts of milk instead of lightning . . .

Now check out Revelation 3:14-21. Don't freak out, Revelation is
not all fantastic creatures and mysterious visions of the end times.
While it certainly deals with unusual images to communicate the
future of God's Kingdom, Revelation also had a very relevant message to Christ-followers when it was written and for us today. Here,
Christ was speaking to seven main churches, providing encouragement or warning. This particular church had grown arrogant,
confident in its own wealth, power, and ability. Jesus said that their
shallow lives made Him sick. The word for "spit" means to "vio-
lently spew". This rich church was so proud of itself that it didn't
recognize the need for God's grace. They left Jesus alone, outside,
too busy to notice Him knocking on the door.

Let's be honest. God knows our deeds. We act like we're doing Him a
favor by saying we believe in Him but going on with our lives, caught
up in pride and possessions, or in the latest fashions and gadgets of
the world. Christ isn't impressed; in fact, it's insulting and sickening.
Jesus isn't looking for lukewarm Christians. He's waiting for
us to open up our lives, welcoming Him all the way in.

REFLECT

1. What do you take great pride in? Is it your looks, your money, your things, your abilities? Do those things cool your passion for God?

2. Is Christ being left out of or welcomed into your life? Your group of friends? How about your church or youth group?

3. Write down the "lukewarm" areas in your own life? These are sneakier than blatant sins, but they still sicken Jesus. Where is your church lukewarm? Where is our culture lukewarm?

VERSE 18

In Minnesota's Mall of America®, there was a unique store called MinneNAPolis. Instead of stuff, the store sold sleep. For 70 cents a minute, weary shoppers could rent a comfortable spot to take a nap! MinneNAPolis included themed rooms such as Asian Mist, Tropical Isle, and Deep Space, with walls thick enough to drown out the squealing children and noisy commotion outside. The company's invitation was simple: "Escape the pressures of the real world into the pleasures of an ideal one." All for just 70 cents a minute! The owner had a rude awakening after only six months when the nap store went out of business.

Jesus offers unlimited rest for free. In Matthew 11:28-30, Jesus invited anyone who's tired and worn out by life's various pressures to come to Him and find rest for their weary souls. In verse 30, Jesus referred to a yoke, which is a wooden crossbeam that links two animals together for carrying a heavy load. The image implies that everyone links up with someone or something to make it easier to plow through life. Anything other than leaning on Christ may provide temporary relief from life's pressures, but ultimately it leaves people tired and empty.

We're tempted to link up with all sorts of things in an attempt to escape from the pressures of life in the real world. Some of us hook up with a boyfriend or a girlfriend. Others depend on an up-to-date wardrobe, extra-curricular activities, or an on-line community. Some even try to lighten things up with alcohol or drugs. But earthly yokes provide no relief in the long run. Although we can't escape life's pressures, we can link our lives with Jesus, the only person capable of sustaining and strengthening life in an unstable, restless world.

1. Which of life's various pressures is most weighing you down at this moment?

2. What yoke are you most tempted to link up with other than Jesus to deal with life's pressures?

3. How will you consistently rely on Jesus for peace and stability in a restless and chaotic world?

SEE TO IT, THEN, THAT THE LIGHT WITHIN YOU IS NOT DARKNESS. *Luke 11:35*

Swirling in controversy, scientists call it the Large Hadron Collider. Other people (like me) call it the Doomsday Machine. It's a mammoth, cement doughnut (16.5 miles around) buried in Europe that is designed to smash particle beams into each other at 99.999999% of the speed of light. All technobabble aside, one thing these brainiacs hope to accomplish is the creation of mini black holes. Once the black hole is formed, it becomes a race against time; can it suck up enough energy to grow before it fades into oblivion? Call me stupid, but if light can't even escape its gravitational force, a bunch of nerds in lab coats trying to birth a black hole and contain it with dirt and concrete doesn't seem so brilliant.

With that haunting your thoughts, read Luke 11:34-36. Jesus often used the opposites of light and darkness to explain spiritual truths and lies, good and evil, understanding and ignorance, or holiness and sin. Here, Christ taught that what enters into people's hearts and minds through their eyes impacts every part of their life.

Looking can (and will) hurt us. What we watch, look at, and see has a greater impact on our spiritual lives than we may realize. Some of us look greedily at material things. For others, it's lustful glances or stares at girls, guys, or images. Whether it's as "serious" as looking at porn, "normal" as reading gossip magazines, or "innocent" as obsessively browsing online stores and window shopping, don't believe the lie that it's ok to look. If we'd be embarrassed or ashamed to tell Jesus what we're looking at and why, then it's darkness. Looking sinfully at things is like creating mini black holes in our souls; that darkness begins to grow, sucking up our energy, until it consumes us . . .

REFLECT

1. What are some things you know you shouldn't read, watch, or look at? Is there anything that you already know is obsessive, like a black hole, consuming your thoughts or time (drowning out God's voice)?

2. How does seeing things influence your thoughts, attitudes, desires, and actions?

3. Write this verse out and put it as a reminder on your computer, locker, mirror, nightstand . . . wherever it will best remind you of God's Word.

VERSE 20

FOR THE KINGDOM OF GOD IS NOT A MATTER OF TALK BUT OF POWER.
1 Corinthians 4:20

Every gymnasium has an unruly group of students who sits close to the court, paints letters on their chests, holds up signs, and stands and screams through an entire basketball game. They chant, cheer, and chastise the opposing team. They're called hecklers. No school has intensified the art of heckling better than Duke University. Known around the country as the Cameron Crazies, the rowdy student section harasses every opposing basketball player who steps into their gym. They look for ways to ridicule the competition. The Cameron Crazies don't take a single minute off from verbally intimidating the other team. But there's a reason why hecklers are in the stands and not on the court. They talk a big game, but they can't hold their own between the lines.

Paul faced a group of hecklers in Corinth, where some posers ridiculed him and his ministry. They said he wouldn't deliver on his promise to visit Corinth. They said Paul was all talk. But in 1 Corinthians 4:20, Paul wrote that God's Kingdom isn't a matter of talk but of power. Therefore, he didn't just talk the talk; he walked the walk. When he arrived in Corinth, his lifestyle convinced everyone that he was in the game following Christ while his opposition was merely heckling from the sidelines. These spectators weren't experiencing life-change because they didn't really believe the gospel, but Paul did, and that makes all the difference.

As Christ-followers, what we believe powerfully changes our lives. What we say about Jesus is confirmed by the difference He makes in us. We don't just talk about the gospel. We're transformed by the gospel. That's the difference between a poser and a player. Christ-followers belong on the court while hecklers stay in the stands. It's not enough to talk a good game if we aren't putting it into action.

reflect

1. Is it possible to believe sincerely in Jesus without experiencing life change? Why or why not?

2. What noticeable difference has believing the gospel made in your life?

3. Where are you "all talk" spiritually? Today, how will you put your faith into action?

VERSE

Does anybody else find it weird to think about a British person faking an American accent? I guess it shouldn't be, but I'm just being honest. English actor Hugh Laurie stars as Dr. Gregory House in FOX's popular series, House™. The drama is a medical mystery inspired by Sherlock Holmes (Homes – House). Each episode involves Laurie's character solving some peculiar case, arriving at unforeseen conclusions through his unique ability to see beyond the surface. The premise of each show is simple: you can't always tell what is really going on inside people just by looking at them. Symptoms are not the real problem; a deeper truth exists.

Read 1 Samuel 16:1-13. In this story, God chose Israel's second king. The original choice was a guy named Saul who looked the part, exactly what people wanted. Eventually his character wavered, and Saul made a string of terrible decisions leading to his political and personal demise. Here, God has sent His prophet to anoint Saul's replacement. Samuel evaluated the young men, determining good candidates for the position, but God had other plans. God was looking for a man after his own heart. David wouldn't prove to be perfect, but he loved God sincerely.

Whether it's how someone is dressed, how they talk, what they drive . . . we judge people all the time. Everything we see is surface however, mostly symptoms of deeper heart conditions. Maybe that neighbor is hurting, or maybe that guy or girl in class is amazing, but we write them off for some reason. Sometimes we play favorites or gravitate toward certain people. Other times we have prejudices, ignoring, avoiding, or excluding people. We're addicted to appearances. God's concern, on the other hand, is the health of our hearts. As part of His Kingdom, we need to start looking at people the same way.

REFLECT

1. What do you think people first notice about you? What would you hope they noticed about you?

2. Knowing that God looks at the heart, what does He see in yours? Is there anything you're embarrassed or ashamed for Him to see? Pray that God would heal those things.

3. Who is someone you may have judged unfairly. Pray for that person and that your heart would be open to knowing him or her better.

VERSE

DO NOT CONFORM ANY LONGER TO THE PATTERN OF THIS WORLD, BUT BE TRANSFORMED BY THE RENEWING OF YOUR MIND. THEN YOU WILL BE ABLE TO TEST AND APPROVE WHAT GOD'S WILL IS—HIS GOOD, PLEASING AND PERFECT WILL. *Romans 12:2*

John Coleman marched in a pipe and drum band during the 2009 presidential inauguration parade. Beforehand, he was warned not to gesture toward anyone in the crowd because it would violate proper etiquette for a military parade. Everyone in the band was expected to stay in sync with one another at all times. However, as Coleman passed the new president of the United States, he refused to ignore him and broke rank. With a wink, a nod, and a wave he acknowledged Barak Obama and was later suspended from the band. For him, acknowledging the president was more important than conforming to the band's code of conduct.

Paul explained the Gospel throughout the first 11 chapters of Romans. Beginning in chapter 12 and continuing to the end of the book, he addressed the transformation that follows salvation. In 12:2, he pointed out that Christians shouldn't walk in sync with the world. Instead of adopting lifestyles that ignore Jesus, Christians break rank from the world by acknowledging Jesus and thinking differently about what's good and enjoyable in life.

The world's code of conduct is promoted everywhere we turn—TV, music, movies, magazines, Internet, etc. The promotion of sex, violence, greed, drunkenness, and self-centeredness bombards us. The pressure to conform our lives to what we see, hear, and read is intense. In order to resist conforming to the pattern of this world, we renew our minds by nurturing our relationship with Jesus. Consider the following suggestions: think about what Jesus did to save you every morning, memorize Scripture, talk with Jesus daily, listen to music that reminds you of Jesus, and try to avoid listening, watching, and reading stuff that doesn't. If Coleman broke rank for the president, how much more willing should we be to get out of step with the pattern of this world for the King of Kings?

1. Is salvation without transformation (real life change) possible? Why?

2. What patterns of this world are you most tempted to keep in step with? Why?

3. How might you renew your mind today?

44

FOR THE KINGDOM OF GOD IS NOT A MATTER OF EATING AND DRINKING, BUT OF RIGHTEOUSNESS, PEACE AND JOY IN THE HOLY SPIRIT. *Romans 14:17*

Dividing lines are sometimes drawn in silly places. Today, many people divide over computers of all things! If you've ever eaten lunch with passionate Mac and PC owners, chances are the conversation turned into a debate over who used the better system. Macers boast in cool graphic capabilities and a compact design. PCers counter with affordability and compatibility. Both sides of the debate look across the aisle with smirks of superiority. Although subtle differences exist between the two computers, ultimately what one chooses boils down to personal opinion.

Read Romans 14. In this chapter, Paul addressed Christians who had divided over matters of opinion. He described one group as "weak." These people didn't eat certain foods. They believed Christians shouldn't eat meat bought in the marketplace because it may or may not have been sacrificed to false gods. Also, they considered certain days more important than others. In contrast, the "strong" group ate everything and considered no day as special believing the life, death, and resurrection of Jesus began a new era. Certain rules no longer applied to God's people. Paul sided with the strong group, but he told them to stop looking down on the weak. Rather than dividing over opinions, both groups would benefit from focusing on righteousness, peace, and joy in the Holy Spirit.

Sometimes dividing lines in churches are drawn in silly places. Some people think certain music styles shouldn't be played in churches. Guitars and drums belong in bars not in church buildings. Others realize God is concerned with musical content not style. Moreover, some say suits and ties rather than jeans and tees are church appropriate when all God cares about is modesty. As Christ-followers, we should agree to disagree about matters of opinion and focus on what clearly matters in the Christian life. Spiritual maturity strives for unity and refuses to fight over silly things.

REFLECT

1. Given that opinions are flexible while facts are not, how might we distinguish between the two in the Christian life?

2. In light of Scripture, identify three clear facts and three matters of opinion (i.e. fact—God demands and desires sexual purity; opinion—Christians should/shouldn't date in high school).

3. Are there certain Christians you look down on because they don't share your opinions on ideas that aren't essential to the Christian faith? How might you continue to love and fellowship with them?

VERSE 24

FOR THOUGH WE LIVE IN THE WORLD, WE DO NOT WAGE WAR AS THE WORLD DOES. *2 Corinthians 10:3*

Remember the round, black, cartoon bomb with the fuse or the stick of dynamite with the ticking alarm clock? You'd laugh as some poor character's eyes would bulge, realizing that he'd been duped. Charred, clothes smoldering, hair singed, the animated victim simply stands there muttering. But we grow up and realize that bombs and warfare are no joke; people don't just walk away. There's a good chance that you know one of the more than 4,000 U.S. troops who have died in Iraq over the past few years. I can almost guarantee that you know somebody, a close friend or family member, who has spent time in the war. It's a big deal. FOX News reports that in 2008, the U.S. spent $188 billion on war.

Check out 2 Corinthians 10:3-5. Here, Paul echoed a thought similar to what Jesus prayed before the crucifixion. Christ prayed that His followers would be in the world but not of it nor taken out of it (John 17:14-20). Paul and Jesus both said that as part of God's Kingdom we still obviously live on this planet, but we cannot live by the standards of our culture or run away from it either.

We are constantly engaged in spiritual warfare. It is a battle for our hearts and minds. But as a follower of Christ, sin has no power over us. Paul says to take every thought captive to the obedience of Christ. Our attitude has to be under the authority of our King; our marching orders are in His Word. Declare war against prideful, selfish, aggressive, and manipulative tendencies in your own life. With Christ in command, we will be victorious. In our own strength, things tend to blow up in our faces. This is a big deal; we need to invest everything in this fight against our flesh.

47

reflect

1. What are some Scriptures (even in this book) that oppose our natural desire to literally fight? Write down what the Bible says about forgiveness, peace, enemies, etc.

2. How could you creatively and biblically deal with situations where you may naturally think an argument, a fight, or even war was unavoidable?

3. What are some strongholds in your own life that need to be knocked down? (sinful thoughts or habits, negative influences, corrupt thinking) Pray for God's help in continually surrendering every thought to Christ.

VERSE

In 2002, Ron Brown was an up-and-coming football coach serving as an assistant at the University of Nebraska. Later that year, he applied for the head coaching job at Stanford University. After the school refused to hire him, they told a Nebraskan newspaper that the coach's Christian faith was a major reason why. Surprisingly, several newspapers around the country applauded Stanford's decision. One writer for a major newspaper in San Francisco stated that the school was right to withhold that position from an outspoken Christian. Not all persecution takes the form of physical abuse and violence. Sometimes it takes the more subtle shape of being shunned.

Read Matthew 5:1-12. Jesus described the kinds of people God blesses because they belong to His Kingdom. The list seems strange. None of Jesus' listeners would have seen persecution as a sign of God's favor. Yet, it's listed as something God blesses. Persecution makes sense given that the total qualities described do not fit well in a world full of aggression, arrogance, and spiritual resistance. Being persecuted becomes an inevitable result for those who adopt the attitudes applauded in God's Kingdom.

As Christ-followers, we shouldn't be surprised when we're treated poorly as a result of our faith. According to Jesus, instead of being sad about it, we should actually be happy. God is pleased when we'd rather be mistreated for the sake of what's right than accepted for the sake of what's wrong. Such faithfulness does not always result in being punched in the face or burned at the stake. In our culture, the more common result is to be kicked out of certain social circles or to be talked bad about. We don't welcome mistreatment, but we don't avoid it either when it comes as a result of being faithful to Jesus.

49

REFLECT

1. Have you ever been mistreated as a result of your faith in Jesus? If so, how did it make you feel?

2. Is it possible to be persecuted for being foolish rather than faithful? If so, in what way?

3. Is pleasing God important to you? How might you grow in your desire to please God?

VERSE 26

SOME TRUST IN CHARIOTS AND SOME IN HORSES, BUT WE TRUST IN THE
NAME OF THE LORD OUR GOD. *Psalm 20:7*

In the spring of 2009, a group of students at Lakeview Elementary School in
a Tennessee town decided to conduct a prayer gathering outside of class time.
They put together a flier for advertising with the words "In God We Trust"
written on the bottom. Before the school administrators allowed the fliers
to be posted, they covered up those words. But is it possible for a Christ-
follower's trust in God to be covered up?

Read Psalm 20. Israel's most adored king, King David, wrote this passage
after having a bad day, the details of which are unknown. In any case, he
reinforced the fact that his trust resided with God. Most people trust in what
they can put their hands on and control. In David's time, most national
rulers trusted in chariots and horses, which were used to win battles. David
also used them to protect Israel from invading armies, but he didn't place
his confidence in them. He knew they could breakdown. Chariots popped
wheels. Horses got sick. There was always an enemy with more resources. But
God stayed steady at all times and through all circumstances. In the midst of
a bad day, David broadcasted to everyone that he still trusted in the reliability
of God.

As Christ-followers, we're tempted to cover up our trust in God by relying
more on what we can put our hands on and control. We live in a world where
people trust in talents, jobs, money, government, etc. But we realize that
such things are unreliable. An athlete can blow out a knee. A job can be lost.
Money can be stolen. The government can make poor decisions. When such
things happen, our peace remains undisturbed because our confidence rests
in the Lord. Therefore, we should broadcast in every circumstance that God
is more reliable than anything else in this world.

51

1. How might a Christ-follower's trust in God be covered up?

2. How do you respond to bad days? Do you consistently turn to the Lord or to something else?

3. How has God proven to be trustworthy and reliable in your life? Pray a prayer thanking Him for being trustworthy and reliable.

Sixty years ago, the White House underwent a serious reconstruction. I'm not talking a remodel; what happened at 1600 Pennsylvania Avenue was truly unique. President Harry S. Truman moved across the street for three years while the presidential home was completely gutted and rebuilt from the inside out. Constant upgrades were tearing the White House apart and adding weight that the frame wasn't intended to support. It was only a matter of time before it would cave in on itself. Truman would joke about the ghosts of former presidents haunting the creaky hallways, but in reality, the building was a deathtrap. When everything was completed, the exterior of the White House still looked the same, but a new strength existed within.

Read Proverbs 14:30. Basically, a proverb is a wise saying; this book is a massive collection of quotes. In biblical times, the technology to acquire information and opportunity to gain an extensive education obviously didn't exist. Loaded with timeless truth, these clever memory devices could be passed from generation to generation. Traditionally believed to be the work of Israel's kings, primarily Solomon, the compilation focuses on how to lead a righteous life.

It's easy for our lives to end up just like the White House, looking great but falling apart. A constant routine of trying to add the next greatest thing to our lives will tear us up. That sick feeling gnaws away at us when we see things we think we need or grow jealous of someone else's possessions, popularity, appearance, or ability. Covering up the truth by putting on a fake smile or showing up to church doesn't fix the problem. (By the way, they removed 40 layers of paint from the crumbling White House!) When content and at peace, we gain an inner strength built on eternity instead of the fading trends of this life.

REFLECT

1. When do you struggle with envy, jealousy, or greed? What things are you especially tempted by? Pray that God would free you from an unhealthy desire for these things.

2. Spend some time acknowledging all of your blessings. This is a great way to fill your heart with peace and contentment.

3. How do you cover up potential problems instead of dealing with them? Today, how will you open the door to let God in for major reconstruction? Be intentional about identifying problem areas and removing them.

VERSE 28

AT THE PRESENT TIME YOUR PLENTY WILL SUPPLY WHAT THEY NEED, SO THAT IN TURN THEIR PLENTY WILL SUPPLY WHAT YOU NEED. THEN THERE WILL BE EQUALITY. *2 Corinthians 8:14*

Be honest. Have you ever cheated playing some board game, tipping that little plastic hourglass over when nobody was looking? You know what I'm talking about. The white sand trickles down, then you flip it so that the top is the bottom and the bottom is the top. There's actually a massive version of this ancient timepiece in Budapest. The 60-ton Timewheel is a work of art commemorating a new beginning in Hungary's history. The monument runs for one full year! When the final granules fall precisely at midnight on New Year's Eve, the Timewheel is rotated 180°.

Read 2 Corinthians 8:7-15. This is the second letter in our Bible that Paul wrote to the church in Corinth. This ancient city was infamous for its self-ish indulgence. The people of Corinth participated in every pleasure their time and money could afford. Here, Paul complimented the generosity of Christ-followers in stark contrast to their culture. People were not only sharing their faith but literally giving their money too. This is the example of Christ, forfeiting what He had in order to bless others. This Scripture reminds that everything someone has can meet someone else's need. God provides enough for everyone; it is simply a matter of man's willingness to share. This practical gesture is a spiritual exercise.

Think back to the hourglass, neither side deserves to be on top or bottom; that is just how it works. Whichever side happens to be on top at the time gives what it has to the other half. When flipped, that half returns the favor. It's a measure of fairness. Imagine what life would be like if we quit feeling entitled to what we have and began sharing and taking turns. It would just work out. God's generosity, giving us His Son, should motivate us to live generously.

reflect

1. What is something you easily share? What is difficult for you to even consider giving away? Why?

2. In what ways do you live like you deserve to be the upper half? Have you ever experienced the other side . . . receiving a generous gift?

3. We have more than we often realize. How could you share with others around you or around the world? Identify what you have "plenty" of and what others "need."

VERSE

Economics isn't the most exciting class in high school. It's sort of like taking cough medicine or getting a shot—hardly anyone likes it, but it is necessary. Whether or not you've taken the class yet, you're probably somewhat aware of the United States' troublesome financial situation. Mom or dad might have complained about the stock market being in bad shape. The stock market can be understood as the pulse of the country's economy. When it's healthy and beating fast, it attracts financial investors. When it's sick and beating slowly, people are more hesitant to invest money. In March 2009, the economy's pulse slowed to a snail's pace. Not many people were comfortable investing their money, fearing it would be a waste. The risk of not receiving a good return was too high.

Read Luke 6:37-38. Jesus taught His followers that God lavishly rewards those who make spiritual investments. At the same time, He warned that God justly responds to those who don't. According to the passage, spiritual investments are made relationally. Christ-followers are expected to treat people a certain way—avoiding harsh and unwarranted criticisms of others, exercising forgiveness when treated poorly, and practicing generosity.

God rewards gestures of kindness, mercy, and generosity because He cares about how we treat people. His passion stems from the fact that as Christ-followers, we are His representatives in the world. The effort we put forth to treat people well and meet their needs says something about what God wants for their lives. By forgiving people, we point to Jesus' forgiveness. By being generous in our time, skills, and resources, we help people realize that God is interested in their well-being. As if the joy of helping people isn't enough, God also promises spiritual rewards in the long run. The only risk is in not making them.

REFLECT

1. How does knowing that God cares about how we treat people affect your approach to relationships?

2. Are you currently making spiritual investments? Why or why not?

3. Take some time and honestly examine how you spend your time, skills, and resources. Does "generous" accurately describe your lifestyle? If not, pray and ask God to give you a generous spirit.

58

VERSE 30

THE KING WILL REPLY, "I TELL YOU THE TRUTH, WHATEVER YOU DID FOR
ONE OF THE LEAST OF THESE BROTHERS OF MINE, YOU DID FOR ME."
Matthew 25:40

Have you ever figured out what it is about a goat that looks sort of creepy? It's not just the gnarly horns or stringy goatee (yep, this is where the trendy chin beard gets its name). It's the eyes; they're square! Well, technically it's their pupils, little rectangular slits across the center of their pale eyes. Apparently this aids in their peripheral depth perception, meaning they have a good sense of what is happening around them.

Read Matthew 25:31-46. This is the final illustration in a string of parables concerning the Kingdom of Heaven and judgment at Christ's return. When standing before His throne, everyone is divided into two groups: sheep and goats. Both ask, "Lord, when did we . . . ?" neither realizing the significance of their past action (or inaction). The surprise testimony in this final judgment is from the King Himself. The evidence presented is the opportunities to love and the action taken (or not taken). What was done for people was done for Jesus; the flipside is also true. Showing grace to others in need (the poor, sick, imprisoned, suffering, lonely) reveals God's grace influencing their own lives. Those belonging to the Kingdom will take care of each other's spiritual, physical, emotional, and material needs. Heaven is real. Hell is too. Sheep go to heaven. Goats . . .

What about us? Are we aware of who and what surrounds us? Do we sense that someone is hurting or recognize practical needs? It is not enough to just say we believe in God's grace. If we really believe, we will be changed from self-centered, religious people to Kingdom-minded servants of Christ. We need to know that what we see around us goes deeper than what meets the eye. Not taking action to meet a need may be the same as ignoring Jesus . . .

1. What needs have you seen around you? Who do you know that is lonely, sick, or suffering in some way? What will you do to comfort them or meet that need?

2. How does seeing everyone around you as Jesus change your attitude or willingness to help them?

3. Right now, based on this story, are you a sheep or goat? Pray for spiritual eyes with the ability to perceive opportunities for sharing God's grace.

verse **31**

The 2007 film Amazing Grace© tells the story of William Wilberforce, a man who followed Christ into the fight against injustice. The cause which seized his soul most severely was slavery. He believed his faith in Christ demanded that he stand up for those unable to stand up for themselves. For more than 40 years, Wilberforce rallied conviction and raised support from people all across 19th century England to end the African slave enterprise. As a result, he's an example of how faith in Christ should fuel efforts to suspend unjust activities in the world, which includes anything that ignores the value of human life.

Read Micah 6:6-8. In the 8th century B.C., the prophet Micah witnessed waves of injustice sweeping across Israel. The wealthy overlooked the needs of the poor. Unfair business practices took advantage of the unsuspecting. Outbursts of violence and abuse occurred often. Meanwhile, so-called worship services took place almost daily. People regularly walked past the oppressed on their way to worship! But Micah called attention to their hypocrisy by reminding them that God wasn't pleased with a faith that ignored the needs of others. Instead, what pleased God is a faith that fueled efforts to help the weak and weary.

Every generation witnesses waves of injustice. Did you know that by the end of this day 30,000 to 60,000 people will have died from hunger alone, and approximately 8,000 will have died in Africa from a preventable disease? Currently, an estimated three million people in the United States are without homes. The list of such wrongs could go on, but you get the picture. Like Wilberforce and Micah, God calls believers in every generation to take action against injustice. In fact, He expects faith in Christ to fuel such efforts and is pleased when they do.

1. Do injustices such as poverty, hunger, and untreated diseases bother you? Why or why not? What weighs most heavily on your heart? What will you do about it?

2. You can become better informed of the needs in your community and around the world by talking with your youth minister or surfing Web sites such as compassioninternational.org. How might you become more involved in meeting the needs you learn about?

3. Download and listen to Charlie Hall's song titled "Micah 6:8" on iTunes®, or take a couple of hours and watch Amazing Grace.

CLOSING

So, how are things different from when you started this book?

Do you have a better picture of just how opposite God's way of thinking and living is from the world's way?

Our hope is that you're seeing straight now. School, parents, friends, stuff . . . life rushes past us at a dizzying speed. The only way to keep from falling is to have a clear focal point, right? To literally flip, you need a point of reference, or you'll get disoriented. Your eyes lock onto a target so that you know when, where, and how to turn. Otherwise, you'll crash. The same is true in your life.

This book was aimed at training your spiritual eyes. If you're not focused on God's Word, you're going to get all mixed up. Fortunately, God loves you like crazy and took radical action to turn your life around.

The exciting thing about flip is that it doesn't end . . . not until all things have been made new. God is still turning people's hearts back to Him.

Can His Kingdom be seen in your life? Stay focused. Remain humble. Be ridiculously generous. As He continues to transform your life, reach out to family, friends, neighbors, strangers, enemies . . . and watch God do what He does . . . FLIP .

ANDREW ARTHUR

Andrew Arthur and his wife, Kim, live in New Orleans, Louisiana. He serves as the lead communicator for Common Ground, a collegiate worship gathering at Tulane University. He also maintains an itinerant preaching ministry in fellowship with Revolution Ministries (revolutionministries.com). He earned a Masters of Divinity from Beeson Divinity School, and he is working towards a Doctorate of Philosophy at New Orleans Baptist Theological Seminary. He spends much of his free time laughing with his wife, hanging out with students, watching baseball, and reading books.

JEREMY MAXFIELD

Jeremy Maxfield makes his home in Birmingham, Alabama, where he lives in a house full of beautiful girls (his wife, Amanda, and their two daughters, Adalyn and Ella). After graduating from the University of Georgia and Beeson Divinity School, he devoted himself to fulltime discipleship as a student minister and small groups pastor. Currently, Jeremy collaborates with the creative minds at Student Life, serving as Resource Development Manager. When not writing, he spends most of his time with his wife, chasing their crazy kids around. They all love listening to good music and being outside.